The Easter Alphabet

by Anne Faulkner

For my god-daughter, Claire, with thanks
for her interest, excitement and encouragement

Text copyright © Anne Faulkner 1999
Illustrations copyright © Zoe Figg 1999
The author asserts the moral right to be identified as the author of this work.
Published by
The Bible Reading Fellowship
First Floor, Elsfield Hall
15–17 Elsfield Way, Oxford OX2 8FG
ISBN 1 84101 033 2
First edition 1999
10 9 8 7 6 5 4 3 2 1
Acknowledgments
Unless otherwise stated, scripture quotations are taken from the Good News Bible
published by The Bible Societies/HarperCollins Publishers Ltd UK © American Bible Society,
1966, 1971, 1976, 1992.
A catalogue record for this book is available from the British Library.
Printed and bound in Malta by Interprint Limited.

Introduction

What kinds of windows do you have in your house? Big ones, small ones, ones with tiny pieces of glass? Ones that open at the top, or at the bottom?

Most of your windows will have clear glass in them, but some windows, especially in churches, have coloured glass, or stained glass. These windows often have tiny pieces of very brightly coloured glass that are made into pictures and patterns.

The Easter Alphabet gives you a chance to make and to colour your own stained-glass window, day by day. But it also helps you to think about what happened to Jesus in the last week of his life on earth—the week we call Holy Week. For each one of the twenty-eight days before Easter you can read a different part of the story, colour in that part of the stained-glass window in the middle of the book and use the special prayer for the day.

By Easter Day you will know what Jesus did in the days leading up to his crucifixion and resurrection, and you will have a complete coloured window to remind you of all that happened.

Using the window as a craft activity

Trace the window shape in the middle of the book on to a sheet of A3 card and, with the help of an adult, cut out along the dotted lines. Trace each picture on to transparent paper and colour it in, then cut it out and stick it behind the window as shown. When your stained-glass window is complete, tape it to the window in your class or bedroom so that the light shines through.

A is for

As Jesus and his disciples approached Jerusalem, they came to Bethphage at the Mount of Olives.

Approaching Jerusalem

Sometimes journeys seem as if they go on for ever. Have you ever been in a car, a bus, a train—or even an aeroplane—and said to an adult with you, 'Are we nearly there yet?' or 'How much longer is it?'

Jesus and his friends had walked the long journey to Jerusalem, and were almost there. As they stood on the hills overlooking Jerusalem, they could see the rooftops, the walls round the city, and the great golden temple glittering in the sun. They were almost there—but not quite—but they had no idea what a happy and sad week they had ahead of them.

A prayer for you to use

Dear God, we do not know what will happen to us today. Help us to remember that you are always with us, when we are happy and when we are sad. Amen

As Jesus came near Bethphage and Bethany at the Mount of Olives, he sent two disciples ahead with these instructions: 'Go to the village there ahead of you...'

B is for Bethphage

Isn't it difficult to do as you are told when you do not understand? Perhaps an adult says, 'Put your toys away, put your coat on and get in the car, please.' You might say, 'Why?' Sometimes adults tell you why, sometimes they don't. It's very easy to answer, 'I don't want to.'

Perhaps the disciples of Jesus wanted to hurry up to get to Jerusalem, but Jesus was telling two of them to go into a nearby village, while he and the other disciples waited. I wonder if they were puzzled or if they knew and trusted Jesus so much after being with him for three years that they did not need to ask why.

A prayer for you to use

Help us, loving Lord, to trust you and to try to listen to what you want us to do. Amen

'...*as you go in, you will find a colt tied up that has never been ridden. Untie it and bring it here. If someone asks you why you are untying it, tell him that the Master needs it.*' *They went on their way and found everything as Jesus had told them.*

C is for Colt

The story gets even more confusing for the disciples. Jesus does tell them why he is sending two of them to the village—to fetch a colt (a young donkey)—but he doesn't tell them what he wants it for.

How do you think they felt as they set off—worried? excited? puzzled? pleased? However they felt, they did as Jesus asked them and they brought the donkey to him. The donkey had never been ridden before, but it did not seem to mind when the disciples helped Jesus to climb on its back.

A prayer for you to use

Dear God, thank you that you used something as ordinary as a donkey to help people to see Jesus. Help us to see Jesus through the ordinary things of life as we work and play. Amen

Luke 19:37

When Jesus came near Jerusalem, at the place where the road went down the Mount of Olives, the large crowd of his disciples began to thank God and praise him in loud voices for all the great things that they had seen.

D *is for* Disciples

I expect that, at home and at school, you have been taught to say 'thank you'. After Christmas and birthdays, you probably have to write thank-you letters. You might not like doing this very much, but it is important to thank others. It's very hurtful and upsetting if we give something to someone, or if we do something for someone, and they take no notice.

When all his friends saw Jesus riding on the back of the donkey, they were filled with joy and happiness and they thanked God very loudly for all that they had seen Jesus do. How happy they were.

A prayer for you to use

Dear God, we are sorry when we forget to thank you for all that you do for us and for all that you give to us. Give us thankful, happy hearts. Amen

6

A large crowd of people spread their cloaks on the road while others cut branches from the trees and spread them on the road.

E *is for* Excitement

What do you do when you get excited? When you are playing an exciting game, or watching a race, or at a party, what do you do? Do you chatter a lot, shout out, jump about?

All the disciples and friends of Jesus were with Jesus as he sat on the donkey going towards the city of Jerusalem. They became very excited and very noisy, shouting out in their happiness, calling him a 'king who comes in the name of the Lord'. They spread their cloaks in the road for the donkey to walk on. Some of the accounts of this story say they cut down branches from the trees (which may have been palm trees) and spread them on the road. What a noise and what a sense of excitement there must have been.

A prayer for you to use

Dear Lord, you are with us all the time. Help us to be excited when we praise you for all your love. Amen

Jesus went into the Temple and drove out all those who were buying and selling there. He overturned the tables of the money-changers and the stools of those who sold pigeons.

F is for Fury

What kinds of things make you cross? What do you do that makes other people cross? Sometimes we are cross and bad-tempered over nothing and we've just 'got out of bed on the wrong side' or are in a bad mood. Sometimes we are cross because we do not get our own way and someone has said 'no'. Sometimes we are cross because something is really wrong.

Jesus wasn't just cross when he came into the Temple at Jerusalem—he was FURIOUS. He was so cross that he went into the Temple market and tipped up all the tables and market stalls of all those who were buying and selling. He was cross—but he was not being bad-tempered. He was right to be cross.

A prayer for you to use

Loving God, please keep us from being bad-tempered and moody when we don't get our own way. Amen

Jesus said to them, 'It is written in the Scriptures that God said, "My Temple will be called a house of prayer." But you are making it a hideout for thieves!'

G is for God's house

Jesus was cross when he drove out those who were buying and selling in the Temple—not because he was in a mood, and not because there was a market in that special holy place. He was cross because they were all cheating—they were charging too much and not giving people enough change when they paid for something. They were not being honest. They were using God's special holy house for stealing and cheating.

God's house is a special place for worship and prayer. We have cathedrals, churches and chapels which are special places for prayer. For Jesus, it was the Temple.

A prayer for you to use

Dear Lord, we thank you for holy places where we can worship you and be near to you in a special way. Amen

The blind and the crippled came to Jesus in the Temple, and he healed them. The chief priests and the teachers of the Law became angry when they saw the wonderful things he was doing and the children shouting in the Temple, 'Praise to David's Son!' So they asked Jesus, 'Do you hear what they are saying?' 'Indeed I do,' answered Jesus. 'Haven't you ever read this scripture? "You have trained children and babies to offer perfect praise."'

H *is for* Hands

Have you ever thought about how we all use our hands? Look at your hands now. You can make them show happiness by clapping or waving; you can make them hurt others by smacking or pushing; you can shake hands with someone to say 'hello'; you can hide your face in your hands if you are crying or if you are shy. Our hands often show how we are feeling.

If we look in this part of the story we hear how Jesus used his hands to heal those who could not see or could not walk. We also hear how some people became angry when they saw Jesus healing people (they may have been shaking their fists with anger). Not everyone was happy with Jesus.

A prayer for you to use

We thank you, loving God, for our hands and for all that we can do with them. Help us to use them with love, kindness and gentleness. Amen

It was now two days before the Festival of Passover and Unleavened Bread. The chief priests and the teachers of the Law were looking for a way to arrest Jesus secretly and put him to death. 'We must not do it during the festival,' they said, 'or the people might riot.' … Then Judas Iscariot, one of the twelve disciples, went off to the chief priests in order to betray Jesus to them. They were pleased to hear what he had to say, and promised to give him money. So Judas started looking for a good chance to hand Jesus over to them.

is for Iscariot

Sometimes we meet people and we find out that they are not very nice, or they are unkind. They are the wrong kind of friends for us to have—they are bad company for us and we should not stay with them.

Judas Iscariot, one of the disciples of Jesus, met some horrid people who wanted to trick and kill Jesus. Although Judas had been a friend of Jesus for three years, he agreed to do as these horrid people wanted. He even took money for doing it. He agreed to let them know when they could have Jesus arrested. He really got himself into bad company. He was not really much of a friend to Jesus after all.

A prayer for you to use

Dear Lord, help us to choose our friends from those who are kind, loyal and loving. Amen

Jesus was in Bethany at the house of Simon, a man who had suffered from a dreaded skin-disease. While Jesus was eating, a woman came in with an alabaster jar full of a very expensive perfume made of pure nard. She broke the jar and poured the perfume on Jesus' head.

J *is for* Jar of perfume

What is the most precious, the most expensive or the most treasured thing that you have? Is it a toy? a book? a piece of jewellery? something you wear? something you were given? I wonder what it is. Ask other people in your house what is their most treasured possession.

For the woman in the story, her most precious possession was a jar or bottle of very expensive perfume. Perhaps she had been keeping it for ages, for a very special occasion. But she poured all the perfume over Jesus' head. In those days that would have been a very special thing to do. She gave it all to him as a gift. She kept none of it for herself and she did not think it was a waste. She wanted to show how much she loved Jesus.

12

A prayer for you to use

It's not always easy, Lord, to think of you rather than ourselves. It is not always easy to be really generous with all that we have. Give us loving hearts. Amen

Then Jesus sent two of his disciples with these instructions: 'Go into the city, and a man carrying a jar of water will meet you. Follow him to the house he enters, and say to the owner of the house: "The Teacher says, Where is the room where my disciples and I will eat the Passover meal?" Then he will show you a large upstairs room, prepared and furnished, where you will get everything ready for us.' The disciples left, went to the city, and found everything just as Jesus had told them.

K is for Knowing

There are lots of things in the world that we do not know about. It's impossible to know everything there is to know—but some people know more than others. I expect you know quite a lot—much more than a small baby or a toddler—but not as much about some things as your teacher or one of your parents.

Because Jesus was so close to God, he often knew things that people around him did not know. He knew that there were people trying to catch him and kill him, he knew that Judas was helping them, and he knew where he and his very close friends would eat a special supper together. So he sent two of his friends to get this supper ready in the upstairs room of a house.

A prayer for you to use

Dear Jesus, you knew that people were trying to trick you and that there were some who wanted to kill you. You could have stopped them, but you did not. Thank you that you did all this for us. Amen

13

While they were eating, Jesus took a piece of bread, gave a prayer of thanks, broke it, and gave it to his disciples. 'Take it,' he said, 'this is my body.' Then he took a cup, gave thanks to God, and handed it to them; and they all drank from it. Jesus said, 'This is my blood which is poured out for many, my blood which seals God's covenant. I tell you, I will never again drink this wine until the day I drink the new wine in the Kingdom of God.'

is for Last Supper

I have a rather old gold watch that belonged to my grandmother. It's not worth very much and it doesn't work any more, but whenever I look at it or think about it I remember my Gran, who died many, many years ago. Perhaps you have something in your home that reminds the family of someone else?

Jesus and his friends sat down to eat the last meal together—the Last Supper. It was the time of a special festival, the Passover, when they were remembering how good God had been over the centuries.

Suddenly Jesus did and said strange things. He took bread and wine and said, 'Eat and drink this in remembrance of me.' He was telling his disciples that, after he had died, whenever they ate bread and drank wine in this way, he would be with them in a special way even though they could not see him. What a gift!

A prayer for you to use

We thank you, heavenly Father, that before Jesus died he gave us a special way to remember him—in bread and wine. Amen

M *is for*

Jesus left the city and went, as he usually did, to the Mount of Olives; and the disciples went with him. When he arrived at the place, he said to them, 'Pray that you will not fall into temptation.' Then he went off from them about the distance of a stone's throw and knelt down and prayed.

Mount of Olives

Most of us sleep in our beds at night. We snuggle down and feel safe and secure in our homes. Even when we go away from home we make sure that we have somewhere to sleep. Jesus did not have a home of his own. He often stayed with friends, but sometimes he slept in the open air. As the weather was usually warm, he would be quite comfortable, but I still don't think I would have liked it very much.

After Jesus and his friends had finished their last supper together, they walked a short distance to a place outside the walls of Jerusalem, where they had been sleeping at night—a place on the Mount of Olives. Instead of settling down to sleep, Jesus told the disciples to stay awake and pray. He went off to pray on his own. He knew that the time would soon come when he would be arrested and killed, but the disciples did not understand and they fell asleep.

A prayer for you to use

15

Thank you, dear God, for the safety and comfort of our homes. We thank you that Jesus was ready to be alone and uncomfortable and we pray for those in our town who have no homes to go to. Amen

Rising from his prayer, he went back to the disciples and found them asleep, worn out by their grief. He said to them, 'Why are you sleeping? Get up and pray that you will not fall into temptation.'

N *is for* Night

Have you ever tried to keep yourself awake when you have been very tired? If you have, you will know how hard it is, and how in the end your eyes close and you fall asleep, even if you don't want to. When it's dark and you can't see anything it's even harder to stay awake. Some people have to work at night and sleep in the day, which must be very muddling for them.

It was night time in our story—it was very late. Some very puzzling, worrying and tiring things had been happening to the friends of Jesus. They had been told by Jesus to pray—but they were too worn out and tired to stay awake any longer. They dropped off to sleep.

A prayer for you to use

Father God, you have given us the night time for rest and sleep. Thank you for those who work while we sleep. Amen

Jesus was still speaking when a crowd arrived, led by Judas, one of the twelve disciples. He came up to Jesus to kiss him. But Jesus said, 'Judas, is it with a kiss that you betray the Son of Man?'

O *is for* Opposition

A kiss is usually a nice thing to give or to get from someone else. We give kisses to those we love, we put kisses in cards and when we write our name at the end of letters. Some kisses say 'hello', some say 'goodbye'. We would not want to kiss someone whom we did not know very well—and may not like very much.

Judas gave Jesus a kiss, but it was not a nice kind of kiss at all. Some of the people who were against Jesus came by night, bringing soldiers to arrest him. Because they did not all know who Jesus was, Judas used a secret sign—a kiss—so that the right person was arrested. It was not a loving kiss, or a kiss that said 'hello', but a kiss that said, 'That's him!' Then they took Jesus away.

A prayer for you to use

Dear God, we thank you for ways of showing love. Help us to love others in our hearts. Amen

They arrested Jesus and took him away into the house of the High Priest; and Peter followed at a distance. A fire had been lit in the centre of the courtyard, and Peter joined those who were sitting round it. When one of the servant-girls saw him sitting there at the fire, she looked straight at him and said, 'This man too was with Jesus!' But Peter denied it, 'Woman, I don't even know him!'

P is for Peter's denial

When I was very small, I whipped my brother's legs with my plastic-covered skipping rope because he was too near my game and I thought he was going to spoil it. I really hurt him and he had red marks all down his legs. When our mother asked what had happened, I pretended I had done nothing. That was very silly, but I was too scared to say I had whipped my brother. Have you ever been too scared to own up to something you have done?

Peter, one of the disciples, was scared too. He had been with Jesus for a long time. He had been part of everything that had happened since they had come to Jerusalem—the donkey ride, the last supper, the arrest of Jesus. And now he was watching from a safe distance to see what was happening to Jesus, but he was SCARED that he too would be in trouble. So when he was asked if he knew Jesus, he said that he didn't.

As Peter spoke, the nearby cockerel crowed, and Jesus turned round and looked at him. How sorry and ashamed Peter was that he had let Jesus down.

A prayer for you to use

Dear Lord, help us to be truthful and to own up when we have done wrong. Help us not to be ashamed to let others know that we love you. Amen

20

Jesus stood before the Roman governor, who questioned him. 'Are you the king of the Jews?' he asked. 'So you say,' answered Jesus. But he said nothing in response to the accusations of the chief priests and elders. So Pilate said to him, 'Don't you hear all these things they accuse you of?' But Jesus refused to answer a single word, with the result that the Governor was greatly surprised.

Q *is for* Questions

Grown-ups are funny about questions. Sometimes they say, 'Ask questions if you want to find out' or, 'It's really good to ask questions' and sometimes they get impatient and say, 'Questions, questions, questions, all you do is ask questions!' But usually we are all encouraged to ask questions, so that we can learn from the answers.

After Jesus had been arrested, he was taken to the Roman Governor, who was called Pontius Pilate. Pilate asked Jesus questions like 'Are you the king of the Jews?' Jesus knew that his enemies did not really want to know the answers. They just wanted to trick him. So he did not really answer, which did not please those who were trying to catch him out.

A prayer
for you to use

Thank you, dear God, for the gentle patience and silence of Jesus when he was accused. Help us to be gentle in what we say to others when they speak unkindly to us. Amen

21

The soldiers took Jesus inside to the courtyard of the governor's palace and called together the rest of the company. They put a purple robe on Jesus, made a crown out of thorny branches, and put it on his head. Then they began to salute him: 'Long live the King of the Jews!'

R *is for* Robe of purple

When Pilate had finished asking Jesus questions, the soldiers took him away. They dressed him up in a purple robe to make him look like a pretend king, and they put a crown made out of thorny branches on his head. Then they laughed at him and made fun of him.

We all know how horrid it is when people laugh at us. We get really upset when people are horrid to us. It must have been just as awful for Jesus, but he said nothing, even though it was all so unfair.

A prayer for you to use

It is sometimes very easy for us to laugh at other people. Dear God, help us to be thoughtful and kind and to treat others as we like to be treated ourselves. Amen

22

 **S** *is for* **Sadness**

Mark 15:24

Then they crucified him and divided his clothes among themselves, throwing dice to see who would get which piece of clothing.

Things got worse for Jesus. The soldiers gave him back his own clothes and then made him carry a cross that was so heavy, he needed help with it. When they reached the space outside the walls of Jerusalem, the soldiers nailed him to the cross. When Jesus was dying, all his friends were very sad and frightened. Most of them were so scared that they ran away. One or two stayed near the cross, not able to do anything, but just to be there watching Jesus die. When we think of Jesus nailed to the cross we feel sad, too.

A prayer for you to use

We thank you, Jesus, that you let yourself be nailed to the cross. We know that it hurt you and that you did it for us. We are sorry that we hurt you sometimes and make you sad when we are naughty or unkind. Amen

With a loud cry Jesus died. … The army officer who was standing there in front of the cross saw how Jesus had died. 'This man was really the Son of God!' he said.

S *is for* Son of God

Do you like Christmas? Of course you do, it's one of the very special times of the year that we look forward to. We remember when Jesus was a tiny baby, born in a stable and laid in a manger. We also remember that angels told the shepherds about his birth, and the wise men followed a special star. Right from the time he was born, Jesus was special because he was God's son.

We are thinking now of Jesus when he was grown up and when he was dying on the cross like a criminal. He was not a criminal although he looked like one to most of the people who were watching by the cross. But as he died, one of the soldiers realized Jesus was special—he was not like other people, he was God's son.

A prayer for you to use

Father God, thank you for your son, Jesus, who was born in Bethlehem and who died on the cross so that we can be sure of how much you love us.
Amen

24

Some women were there, looking on from a distance. Among them were Mary Magdalene, Mary the mother of the younger James and of Joseph, and Salome. They had followed Jesus while he was in Galilee and had helped him. Many other women who had come to Jerusalem with him were there also.

S is for Some women

We tend to think of the friends of Jesus as being men—Peter, Andrew, John—but when Jesus died there were some women there too, watching and waiting some way away from the cross.

When we are sad or when we are hurting, our mother can be one of the people who helps us most. We know that most mothers care, we know that they want to help.

So we are not surprised that one of the women who watched as Jesus died would have been his mother, Mary. How sad that must have been for her.

A prayer for you to use

Father, we remember how the women
sadly waited and watched while Jesus died.
We thank you for their love and we pray
that we may love you more. Amen

Joseph brought a linen sheet, took the body down, wrapped it in the sheet, and placed it in a tomb which had been dug out of solid rock. Then he rolled a large stone across the entrance to the tomb.

T is for **Tomb**

Do you have kind friends who are there to help you? What sort of things do they do for you? Do they chat to you? cheer you up? share their toys? invite you to sleep over?

One of Jesus' friends did something very special for him. This friend was called Joseph of Arimathea. When Jesus died, Joseph asked to have the body of Jesus. He took it down from the cross, wrapped it in a clean sheet and laid it in a tomb in a hollowed-out rock. What a kind and lovely thing to do for Jesus.

A prayer for you to use

Dear Jesus, just when you needed a friend, Joseph came to help. Please give us the love to be generous friends when others need us. Amen

'Take a guard,' Pilate told them; 'go and make the tomb as secure as you can.' So they left and made the tomb secure by putting a seal on the stone and leaving the guard on watch.

U *is for* Under orders

Not everyone was sad that Jesus had died. The people who had been against him for a long time were pleased that he was dead, and that they would not have to listen to him any more. But they were worried that Jesus' friends would steal his body, so Pilate ordered a great big stone—so big it probably took several men to move it—to be put in front of the entrance to the tomb in the rock. Pilate also ordered some of the soldiers to stand guard and watch the tomb.

A prayer for you to use

Dear God, help us always to be kind and loving and to see good in others. Please help us never to be secretly pleased if horrid things happen to people we don't like very much. Amen

Early on Sunday morning, while it was still dark, Mary Magdalene went to the tomb and saw that the stone had been taken away from the entrance. She went running to Simon Peter and the other disciple, whom Jesus loved, and told them, 'They have taken the Lord from the tomb, and we don't know where they have put him!'

is for **Very early**

Have you ever woken up very early in the morning? So early that it is not really light, so early that the street outside, or your garden, is very still and quiet (unless you live in a very busy town)? It can be a very special time of the day, especially if we sit and listen.

It was very early one morning, soon after Jesus had died, that one of his friends, Mary Magdalene, came to his tomb in the garden. It was still dark and she was sad, but it turned out to be a special morning for her. Quickly she realized that the big stone had gone from the front of the tomb and that the cave was empty. She ran as fast as she could to tell the other friends of Jesus that he had gone.

A prayer for you to use

We thank you, loving God, for all the various times of the day. Help us to notice how different they can be: the early morning is so different from the evening, the middle of the day is different from the night time. Each time is special. Thank you. Amen

Then Peter and the other disciple went to the tomb. The two of them were running, but the other disciple ran faster than Peter and reached the tomb first. He bent over and saw the linen wrappings, but he did not go in. Behind him came Simon Peter, and he went straight into the tomb. He saw the linen wrappings lying there and the cloth which had been round Jesus' head. ... Then the other disciple, who had reached the tomb first, also went in; he saw and believed.

W *is for* Wonder

I have just had e-mail fitted to my computer. I know that if I press certain keys and buttons, I can send and receive messages, but I do not really understand it. There are many things in life that we do not understand, or that we only half understand.

So it was with the disciples. Peter and John came to the tomb when Mary Magdalene told them the body of Jesus had gone. They stooped down and went inside. They saw the cloths that Jesus had been wrapped in. They wondered that he was not there—yet, they did not really understand what had happened.

A prayer for you to use

Father God, we do not always understand your world, or what you do, but help us to trust you and to wonder, and to believe in you. Amen

29

Mary stood crying outside the tomb … Then she turned round and saw Jesus standing there; but she did not know that it was Jesus. 'Woman, why are you crying?' Jesus asked her. 'Who is it that you are looking for?' She thought he was the gardener, so she said to him, 'If you took him away, sir, tell me where you have put him, and I will go and get him.' Jesus said to her, 'Mary!' She turned towards him and said in Hebrew, 'Rabboni!' (This means 'Teacher'.)

X *is for* The love of God

Think about what happens when we cry. It's hard to think properly because of the tears, it's hard to speak because of the sobs. We can feel very miserable and alone.

That's how Mary Magdalene felt. Peter and John went home, the tomb was empty, the garden was quiet, she was so sad. Her friend Jesus had gone. She was sure that someone had stolen his body and she stood and cried and cried.

She was so upset that when a man came towards her she thought he was the gardener. Only when the man called her by her name, 'Mary', did she realize it was Jesus. He was alive. He was risen from the dead.

A prayer for you to use

Oh God, thank you for loving us so much that Jesus came to earth, died for us and rose from the dead. Help us to hear when he calls us by name and to love him. Amen

Y is for Yes

It was late that Sunday evening, and the disciples were gathered together behind locked doors, because they were afraid of the Jewish authorities. Then Jesus came and stood among them. 'Peace be with you,' he said. After saying this, he showed them his hands and his side. The disciples were filled with joy at seeing the Lord. Jesus said to them again, 'Peace be with you. As the Father sent me, so I send you.'

What are you scared of? Is it the dark? or spiders? or thunderstorms? or some TV programmes? Do you run and hide behind the sofa? hide your eyes? put your head under the duvet? or what?

The disciples were scared of the enemies of Jesus. They were so frightened that they locked themselves in a room together so that no one could catch them. They locked the doors and the windows so that no one could get in.

And then Jesus was there with them. Mary had seen him in the garden and now he came to his other special friends. They were so pleased to see him alive again. He showed them the places in his hands where the nails had been and the wound in his side from the soldier's spear. They could hardly believe it—but YES, it was JESUS—he had risen from the dead.

A prayer for you to use

Thank you, Jesus, for all that you suffered and for rising from the dead. We want to believe in you and we want to follow you. Amen

31

'Go, then, to all peoples everywhere and make them my disciples: baptize them in the name of the Father, the Son, and the Holy Spirit, and teach them to obey everything I have commanded you. And I will be with you always, to the end of the age.'

Z is for Alpha † and Omega

How old are you? How old are your brothers and sisters? your friends? your relatives? Even if you added together the ages of all the members of your family or all the people in your class at school, it would not come to a very big number. It would not be many years altogether. Perhaps it might be a few hundred or even a thousand.

We do not think of God as so many years old. He created the universe, and he made everything in our world. He gave people brains and understanding so that they could discover and invent all kinds of clever things, and learn more and more new ideas. God has always been there—and he always will be there.

Jesus told his disciples that he would always be with them even when they could no longer see him.

A prayer for you to use

Thank you, Father God, for always being with us. Thank you for Jesus who always loves us. Thank you for the Holy Spirit who always guides and helps us. Amen